Will You Be My Ring Bearer?

Ring Bearer Coloring Book for Celebrating Little Boys Special Role

Cover and page design by Cool Journals Studios - Copyright 2018

Dear _____

You're a darling little boy
who melts our hearts away
please do us this kindness and
join us on our wedding day

Will you be our ring bearer?

Love,

Signed_____ Date_____

THE RING BEARER PLAYS AN IMPORTANT ROLE.

THE RING BEARER IS CAREFUL WITH THE RING.

THE RING BEARER KEEPS THE RING SAFE.

THE RING BEARER GETS DRESSED.

THE RING BEARER SOMETIMES WEARS A VEST.

THE RING BEARER SOMETIMES WEARS SUSPENDERS.

THE RING BEARER SOMETIMES WEARS A NECK TIE.

THE RING BEARER SOMETIMES WEARS A BOW TIE.

THE RING BEARER SOMETIMES WEARS A BOUTONNIERE.

THE RING BEARER IS COOL.

THE RING BEARER KEEPS THE RINGS TOGETHER.

THE RING BEARER SOMETIMES HAS A BOX FOR THE RING.

THE RING BEARER SOMETIMES HAS A PILLOW FOR THE RING.

THE RING BEARER WALKS DOWN THE AISLE.

THE RING BEARER STANDS NEXT TO THE FLOWER GIRL.

THE RING BEARER TAKES PICTURES WITH THE GROOM.

THE RING BEARER TAKES PICTURES WITH THE BRIDE.

THE RING BEARER EATS CAKE.

THE RING BEARER DANCES.

THE RING BEARER HAS FUN.

Let's Draw.

Let's Draw.

Let's Draw.

Let's Draw.

Let's Draw.

Draw your face.

WHICH BOX MATCHES THE PICTURE?

a

b

c

your answer

WHICH BOX MATCHES THE PICTURE?

a

b

c

your answer

MATCH THE RING BEARER TO HIS SHADOW.

A

B

C

MATCH THE RING BEARER TO HIS SHADOW.

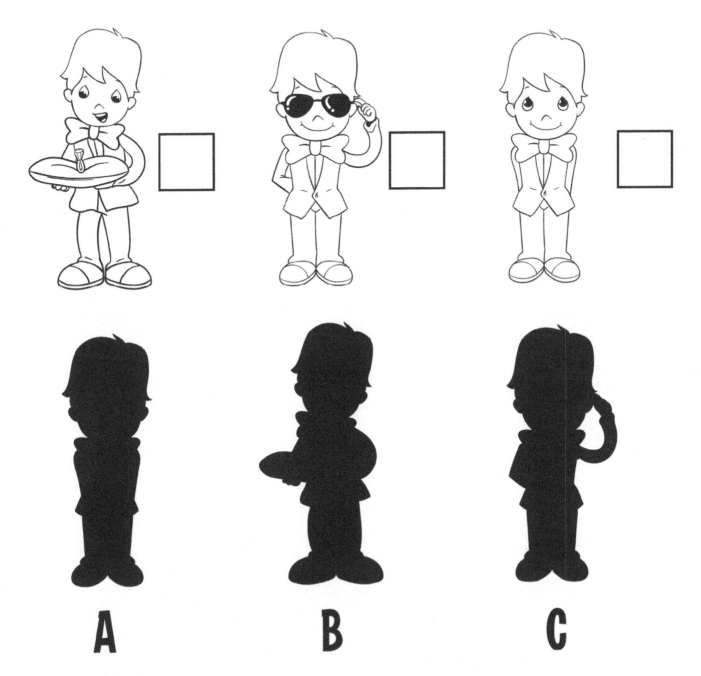

Find the ring bearer that is different from the rest.

FIND THE RING BEARER THAT IS DIFFERENT FROM THE REST.

FIND THE RING BEARER THAT IS DIFFERENT FROM THE REST.

FIND THE RING BEARER THAT IS DIFFERENT FROM THE REST.

FIND THE RING BEARER THAT IS DIFFERENT FROM THE REST.

My Day as the Ring Bearer

I wore...

I saw...

My favorite part of being dressed up...

My Day as the Ring Bearer

I ate...

I met...

My favorite part of the reception...

My Day as the Ring Bearer

I smelled...

I heard...

My favorite part of the day...

My Day as the Ring Bearer

I touched...

I played...

My favorite part of the wedding...

What a great day!

attach a picture of the wedding
couple and the ring bearer here

Made in the USA
Las Vegas, NV
10 February 2024

85607095R00050